Reading Skill Competency Tests

FIRST LEVEL

Henriette L. Allen, Ph.D.

Henriette L. Allen, Ph.D., is a former classroom teacher in the schools of Coventry, Rhode Island, the Aramco Schools of Dhahran, Saudi Arabia, The American Community School of Benghazi, Libya, and Jackson, Mississippi. Dr. Allen served in several administrative roles, including assistant superintendent of the Jackson Public Schools. She is presently an education consultant recognized nationally. Dr. Allen is the senior author of the series *Competency Tests for Basic Reading Skills* (West Nyack, NY: The Center for Applied Research in Education). She has taught reading skills at both elementary and secondary levels, has supervised the development of a Continuous Progress Reading Program for the Jackson Public Schools, and has lectured widely in the fields of reading, classroom management, technology in the classroom, and leadership in educational administration. Dr. Allen is listed in the *World Who's Who of Women* and *Who's Who—School District Officials*. She was the 1996 recipient of the Distinguished Service Award given by the American Association of School Administrators.

Walter B. Barbe, Ph.D.

A nationally known authority in the fields of reading and learning disabilities, Walter B. Barbe, Ph.D., was for twenty-five years editor-in-chief of the widely acclaimed magazine *Highlights for Children,* and adjunct professor at The Ohio State University. Dr. Barbe is the author of over 150 professional articles and a number of books, including *Personalized Reading Instruction* (West Nyack, NY: Parker Publishing Company, Inc.), coauthored with Jerry L. Abbot. He is also the senior author and editor of two series—*Creative Growth with Handwriting* (Columbus, OH: Zaner-Bloser, Inc.) and *Barbe Reading Skills Check Lists and Activities* (West Nyack, NY: The Center for Applied Research in Education)—and he is senior editor of *Competency Tests for Basic Reading Skills.* Dr. Barbe is a fellow of the American Psychological Association and is listed in *Who's Who in America* and *American Men of Science.*

Wiley C. Thornton, M.Ed.

Wiley C. Thornton, M.Ed., is experienced in classroom teaching and educational testing and is the former research assistant in the Jackson Public Schools. His responsibilities include project evaluations, report writings, upgrading of teacher skills in interpretation and use of educational research, as well as test construction. Mr. Thornton was a frequent consultant and speaker to teacher, parent, and civic groups on educational measurement, testing, and test construction and use.

COMPETENCY TESTS FOR BASIC READING SKILLS
The Center for Applied Research in Education
West Nyack, New York 10994

Library of Congress Cataloging-in-Publication Data

Allen, Henriette L.
  Reading Skills Competency Tests : competency tests for basic
reading skills / Henriette L. Allen, Walter B. Barbe, Brandon B.
Sparkman.
    p.   cm.
  Wiley C. Thornton is named as third author on title pages of v.
2-5.
  Contents: [1] Readiness level — [2] First level — [3] Second
level — [4] Third level — [5] Fourth level — [6] Fifth level —
[7] Sixth level — [8] Advanced level.
  ISBN 0-13-021325-X (v. 1). — ISBN 0-13-021326-8 (v. 2). — ISBN
0-13-021327-6 (v. 3). — ISBN 0-13-021328-4 (v. 4). — ISBN
0-13-021329-2 (v. 5). — ISBN 0-13-021331-4 (v. 6). — ISBN
0-13-021332-2 (v. 7). — ISBN 0-13-021333-0 (v. 8).
  1. Reading Skills Competency Tests. 2. Reading—Ability testing.
I. Barbe, Walter Burke. II. Sparkman, Brandon B.
III. Title. IV. Title: Competency tests for basic readingskills.
LB1050.75.R43A45   1999
372.48—dc21   98-51643
                                                       CIP

© 1999 by The Center for Applied Research in Education, West Nyack, NY

Printed in the United States of America

10 9 8 7 6 5 4 3 2 1

ISBN 0-13-021326-8

ATTENTION: CORPORATIONS AND SCHOOLS

The Center for Applied Research in Education books are available at quantity discounts
with bulk purchase for educational, business, or sales promotional use. For information,
please write to: Prentice Hall Special Sales, 240 Frisch Court, Paramus, NJ 07652. Please
supply: title of book, ISBN number, quantity, how the book will be used, date needed.

THE CENTER FOR APPLIED RESEARCH
IN EDUCATION
West Nyack, NY 10994

On the World Wide Web at http://www.phdirect.com

PRENTICE-HALL INTERNATIONAL (UK) LIMITED, *LONDON*
PRENTICE-HALL OF AUSTRALIA PTY. LIMITED, *SYDNEY*
PRENTICE-HALL CANADA INC., *TORONTO*
PRENTICE-HALL HISPANOAMERICANA, S.A., *MEXICO*
PRENTICE-HALL OF INDIA PRIVATE LIMITED, *NEW DELHI*
PRENTICE-HALL OF JAPAN, INC., *TOKYO*
PEARSON EDUCATION ASIA PTE. LTD., *SINGAPORE*
EDITORA PRENTICE-HALL DO BRASIL, LTDA., *RIO DE JANEIRO*

About the *Competency Tests for Basic Reading Skills*

The Reading Skills Competency Tests are a practical tool designed to provide classroom teachers, reading specialists, Title I teachers and others an inventory of those reading skills mastered and those which need to be taught. The tests can be used at all levels with any reading program, as they test mastery of specific reading skills at particular levels.

For easiest use, the test materials are organized into eight distinct units tailored to evaluate children's reading skills at each of the following expectancy and difficulty levels:

Reading Skills Competency Tests: READINESS LEVEL
Reading Skills Competency Tests: FIRST LEVEL
Reading Skills Competency Tests: SECOND LEVEL
Reading Skills Competency Tests: THIRD LEVEL
Reading Skills Competency Tests: FOURTH LEVEL
Reading Skills Competency Tests: FIFTH LEVEL
Reading Skills Competency Tests: SIXTH LEVEL
Reading Skills Competency Tests: ADVANCED LEVEL

The tests give reading teachers a quick, informal means to measure the mastery of reading objectives. They can be used at any time to assess the student's competence in specific reading skills, to pinpoint specific skill weaknesses and problems, and to plan appropriate corrective or remedial instruction in an individualized reading program.

The sequence of the tests corresponds to the sequence of the well-known "Barbe Reading Skills Check Lists," which provide a complete developmental skill sequence from Readiness through Advanced Levels. Each level-unit presents ready-to-use informal tests for evaluating all skills that are listed on the Skills Check List at that level. Tests can be administered individually or to a group by a teacher or a paraprofessional.

Each unit of test materials contains:

1. Directions for using the *Reading Skills Competency Tests* at that grade level to identify individual reading needs and prescribe appropriate instruction.

2. Copies of the Skills Check List and a Group Summary Profile at that grade level for use in individual and group recordkeeping.

3. Reading Skills Competency Tests for assessing all skills at that particular grade level, including teacher test sheets with directions and answer keys for administering and evaluating each test plus reproducible student test sheets.

4. A copy of the "Barbe Reading Skills Sequential Skill Plan" chart.

For easy use of the materials, complete directions are provided in each unit for using the Competency Tests at that level and for recording the information on the student skills Check List and the Group Summary Profile.

The test items in each level-unit correspond to the skills indicated on the Check List. The Check List can be marked to indicate which skills the child has mastered or the skills in which further instruction is needed. The Group Summary Profile can be used to obtain an overall picture of class progress and to identify the skills which need to be taught. It is also useful in identifying small groups with similar needs, students who require personalized help on a prerequisite skill, and students who need continued help on a current skill.

You will find that these tests provide for:

- quick, informal assessment of students' competence in reading skills
- diagnosis and prescription of specific reading skill weaknesses and needs
- devising of appropriate teaching strategies for individuals and small or large groups
- continuous evaluation of each child's progress in the basic reading skills
- flexibility in planning the reading instructional program
- immediate feedback to the student and the teacher

The Competency Tests for Basic Reading Skills can be used by all reading teachers in either a self-contained classroom or a team setting. They are as flexible as the teacher chooses to make them. Hopefully, they will provide an efficient, systematic means to identify the specific reading skills that students need to learn and thus meet, to a greater degree, their individual reading needs.

Henriette L. Allen

Walter B. Barbe

Contents

How to Use the Competency Tests and Check List

A major task for teachers is verifying mastery of basic skills and keeping records. Recordkeeping and competency tests are of greater concern today than ever before. But knowing of their necessity does not make the task any easier. Competency tests and the accompanying records may be compared to a road map. One must drive through Town B to reach Town W. Competency tests are designed to assist you in verifying mastery of basic reading skills, and to indicate where to begin on the journey of reading mastery. The Reading Skills Check Lists provide check points to verify (1) where the student is on the sequence of skills, (2) when the skills were mastered, and (3) at what rate he or she is progressing.

In order for skills to develop sequentially, it is vital that we have an idea of where a student is within the sequence of reading skills. The Reading Skills Competency Tests and Check List in this unit are designed to help you teach directly to identified student needs, on a day-to-day, week-to-week, and month-to-month basis.

The Reading Skills Competency Tests are easy-to-administer tests for each reading skill on the "Barbe Reading Skills Check Lists." Directions for administering each test are given on a teacher page. This page also provides the answer key and the number of correct responses needed for mastery. Facing the teacher page is the student test page, which can be used as a master for copying when reproduction for classroom use is via copy machine.

The Check Lists are not intended as a rigid program for reading instruction. Rather they are meant to provide a general pattern around which a program may be built. The First Level Skills Check List is divided into four major headings: Vocabulary, Word Analysis, Comprehension, and Oral and Silent Reading Skills. Each area is of great importance to the student's development. In presenting the skills on the Check List, it is recommended that you deal alternately with some activities from each of the four major headings.

You will find a copy of the First Level Skill Check List on page 14, which you can copy and use for individual recordkeeping.

Begin at the Beginning

Before planning an instructional program for any pupil, it is necessary to determine at what level the student is reading. This may be determined through the use of an informal reading inventory. It is then necessary to identify which basic reading skills the pupil has mastered and which skills need remediation or initial teaching.

The Competency Tests for Basic Reading Skills offer a quick, practical means to determine which skills the student has mastered and on which the student needs additional work. It is suggested that the tests be administered at the beginning of a school year. The tests may also be used at any time throughout the year to determine a student's entry point in a Reading Skills Class, or to reevaluate the progress of individual students. The tests may be given to a large group, a small group, or an individual, whichever is appropriate for those being tested and for the test being administered. Some tests, such as Oral Reading, must be administered individually. The entry point into the reading program should be at that point when a student begins to encounter difficulty with a particular reading skill.

The tests may be used as a pre test to indicate where instruction is needed, and the same tests may also be used as a post test to indicate mastery or non-mastery. Once a pupil's areas of difficulty are identified, you may then plan instructional activities accordingly. After the student has worked through a unit of instruction, you may use the same test to verify mastery of the skill. When mastery occurs, the student is advanced to another skill. When the student is unsuccessful on the specific test item, additional instruction is needed. If a reasonable amount of instruction does not result in mastery, it may be that changing instructional approaches is needed or that more work is needed on earlier skills.

Once you have decided the level of mastery tests needed, the assessing part of the reading program is ready to begin. Specific directions are given for each test. At the First Level, it is recommended that you give all directions orally. The directions for the test and what you may say to the students is on every teacher page. In some instances, as in oral reading, you may have to test each student individually.

Recording on the Check List

Recordkeeping is an important part in any instructional design. Simplicity and ease is vital. One effective method for marking Skills Check List is as follows:

III. Comprehension
    A. Understands that printed symbols represent
       objects or action
    B. Can follow printed directions
    C. Can draw conclusions from given facts
    D. Can recall from stories read aloud:
       1. Main idea
       2. Names of characters
       3. Important details
       4. Stated sequence
    E. Can recall after silent reading:
       1. Main idea
       2. Names of characters
       3. Important details
       4. Stated sequence

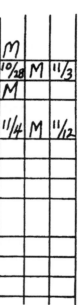

Put an M in the first column if the pupil takes a test and demonstrates mastery of that basic reading skill. If the pupil has not mastered the skill, record the date. The date in column one indicates when instruction in the skill began. When the pupil is tested a second time, put an M in the second column if mastery is achieved, and record the date of mastery in the third column. Thus, anyone looking at the Check List can tell if the student mastered the skill before instruction or when instruction began, and when the skill was actually mastered. The Check List provides a written record of: (1) where the student is on the sequence of reading skills, (2) when the student mastered the skills, and (3) at what rate the student is progressing.

Conferencing with the Pupil

The student and teacher may discuss performance on the Competency Tests and Check List and jointly plan subsequent instruction. The Check List provides a guide for this discussion.

Conferencing with Parents

The Reading Skills Check List also serves as a guide for parent conferences. Using the Check List you can talk with parents about specific skills mastered, as well as those which have been taught but not yet fully mastered. Use of the Check List reassures parents of your concern for skill instruction, your knowledge of ways to aid their child in becoming a better reader, and of your professional plan which considers each child individually.

Conferencing with Professional Staff

Conferences with other staff such as school psychologists, counselors, and principals concerning an individual child's reading progress should focus on the instructional plan. When Check Lists are used, other professional staff members are provided with a written record of the teacher's progress and the child's progress in this program. The Check List provides information on the skills mastered, and when the skills were mastered.

Providing Check Lists to the Next Grade Level Teacher

One of the great problems in teaching reading skills at the beginning of the year is to know where to begin. If the Reading Skills Check Lists are passed along from class to class, the new teacher will know the skill level of every student in the room.

Making a Group Summary Profile from Individual Check Lists

While the Reading Skills Check List is intended primarily for individual use, there are various reasons for bringing together a record of the instructional needs of the entire class. In planning classroom strategies, you will find the use of the Group Profile on pages 16 and 17 helpful.

After you have recorded the skill level for each student on the Reading Skills Check List, you may then enter this information on the Group Profile. The Group Summary Profile is designed to help you identify groups of students who need a particular skill. It is a visual representation of the instructional needs of the entire class. It also presents the specific strengths and achievement levels of individual students.

The Group Profile may be used in conferences with supervisors and administrators to discuss the status of a particular class, the point of initial instruction, and the progress made to date. A different colored pen or pencil may be used to indicate the different grading or marking periods of the school year. This further indicates the progress the pupils have made within these periods of time.

The Group Profile can indicate the instructional materials and supplies which are needed. Since specific reading skills needs will be clearly identified, materials may be purchased which meet these needs.

Ensuring the Sequential Presentation of Skills

One of the goals of reading instruction is to develop a love of reading. But if students are to develop a love of reading, they must be able to read with efficiency. And in order to be efficient readers they must have at their ready command all of the necessary skills, including the ability to unlock new words and to read rapidly.

If the skills are to be mastered, they must be presented sequentially. When skills are presented out of sequence, critical skills are in danger of being bypassed or given minimal attention.

In many instances, the sequence of skills is firmly established; in other instances the sequence is less rigid. In these Check Lists, the skills have been placed in the order the authors feel is logical. Teachers should be free to change this sequence when there is reason to do so, being careful not to eliminate the presentation of the skill.

It is important that some skill instruction be conducted in groups. This prevents individual students from becoming isolated, a danger which sometimes occurs when too much individualization is undertaken.

Using the Sequential Skill Plan Chart

The importance of viewing the total sequential skills program cannot be minimized. The chart is intended primarily for use by the classroom teacher. If a personalized approach is used in teaching reading skills, it is still essential that the teacher view the skills as a continuous progression rather than as skills for a specific grade level. This chart allows the teacher to view not only those skills that are taught principally at the present grade placement, but also those skills which will be taught as the student progresses.

As an inservice tool, the chart provides teachers with the opportunity to see their own positions in the skills progression. It should be understood, of course, that there are any number of reasons why decisions may be made to teach the skills at levels different from those indicated on the chart. But it is important that reading skills be taught, and that basically they be taught in a sequential manner, in a planned reading program. Incidental teaching of reading skills often results in vital skills being neglected, or being bypassed until the student encounters difficulties. At that point, having to go back to earlier skills is more difficult and less effective.

The chart also provides administrators, supervisors, and teachers with direction for a total skills program.

Reading Skills Check List— First Level

On the following pages you will find a copy of the "Barbe Reading Skills Check List— First Level." The Check List presents a sequential outline of the skills to be mastered at this level in four major areas: Vocabulary, Word Analysis, Comprehension, and Oral and Silent Reading.

You may photocopy the First Level Skills Check List as many times as you need it for use in individual recordkeeping.

Accompanying this unit is a copy of the "Barbe Reading Skills Check List Sequential Skill Plan." This chart provides a visual representation of the total reading skills progression through all levels, including:

Readiness Level

First Level

Second Level

Third Level

Fourth Level

Fifth Level

Sixth Level

Advanced Level

BARBE READING SKILLS CHECK LIST
FIRST LEVEL

(Last Name)　　　　(First Name)　　　　(Name of School)

(Age)　　　(Grade Placement)　　　(Name of Teacher)

I. Vocabulary:
Word Recognition
1. Recognizes words with both upper and lower-case letters at beginning
2. Knows names of letters in sequence
3. Is able to identify in various settings the following words usually found in preprimers and primers:

___ a	___ eat	___ look	___ TV
___ about	___ farm	___ make	___ table
___ again	___ father	___ man	___ take
___ all	___ fast	___ many	___ thank
___ am	___ find	___ may	___ that
___ an	___ fine	___ me	___ the
___ and	___ fish	___ mitten	___ their
___ apple	___ for	___ mother	___ them
___ are	___ from	___ more	___ then
___ as	___ fun	___ morning	___ there
___ at	___ funny	___ must	___ they
___ away	___ get	___ my	___ this
___ baby	___ girl	___ near	___ tree
___ back	___ give	___ new	___ to
___ ball	___ go	___ night	___ too
___ be	___ good	___ no	___ toy
___ bed	___ good-by	___ not	___ two
___ been	___ green	___ of	___ up
___ big	___ has	___ on	___ up
___ birthday	___ had	___ one	___ walk
___ black	___ happy	___ or	___ want
___ blue	___ have	___ party	___ was
___ boat	___ he	___ pie	___ water
___ boy	___ help	___ play	___ way
___ but	___ her	___ pretty	___ we
___ by	___ here	___ puppy	___ went
___ cake	___ hide	___ put	___ were
___ call	___ him	___ rabbit	___ what
___ came	___ his	___ ran	___ when
___ can	___ home	___ red	___ where
___ car	___ house	___ ride	___ which
___ Christmas	___ how	___ run	___ white
___ come	___ I	___ said	___ who
___ cookies	___ if	___ sat	___ will
___ could	___ in	___ saw	___ wish
___ cow	___ is	___ see	___ with
___ cowboy	___ it	___ she	___ woman
___ daddy	___ jump	___ show	___ work
___ day	___ just	___ sleep	___ would
___ did	___ kitten	___ so	___ yellow
___ dinner	___ know	___ some	___ yes
___ dish	___ laugh	___ something	___ you
___ do	___ let	___ soon	___ your
___ dog	___ like	___ splash	
___ down	___ little	___ stop	
	___ long	___ surprise	

II. Word Analysis:
A. Sound-symbol Associations
1. Associates consonant sounds to the following letters:

b	___	h	___	n	___	t	___
c (cat)	___	j	___	p	___	v	___
d	___	k	___	q	___	w	___
f	___	l	___	r	___	y	___
g	___	m	___	s	___	z	___

2. Names letters to represent consonant sounds heard in:
   initial position
   final position
   medial position

3. Discriminates between words using:
   initial letter cues
   (Which word is hat? hat-foot)
   final letter cues
   (Which word is bear? bear-boat)
4. Associates sounds to digraphs:
   sh ___　th (this and thin ___
   wh ___　ch (church)
5. Associates sounds to two letter blends:

st ___	fr ___	gr ___	sw ___
bl ___	fl ___	sp ___	br ___
pl ___	cl ___	sm ___	gr ___
tr ___	gl ___	sn ___	sl ___

6. Knows that the letters a, e, i, o, u, and combinations of these can represent several different sounds

B. Structural Analysis
1. Knows endings
   ed sound as "ed" in wanted
   ed sound as "d" in moved
   ed sound as "t" in liked
2. Recognizes compound words
   (into, upon)
3. Knows common word families

all ___	an ___	ell ___	ook ___	in ___
at ___	ill ___	ay ___	ing ___	ish ___
it ___	et ___	ake ___	ack ___	ight ___

C. Word Form Clues
1. Recognizes upper and lower-case letters
2. Recognizes words of different length
3. Recognizes words with double letters

III. Comprehension
A. Understands that printed symbols represent objects or actions
B. Can follow printed directions
C. Can draw conclusions from given facts
D. Can recall from stories read aloud:
   main idea
   names of characters
   important details
   stated sequence
E. Can recall after silent reading:
   main idea
   names of characters
   important details
   stated sequence
F. Can distinguish between real and imaginary events
G. Uses context clues in word attack
H. Can suggest or select an appropriate title for a story
I. Can relate story content to own experiences

IV. Oral and Silent Reading Skills:
A. Oral Reading
1. Uses correct pronunciation
2. Uses correct phrasing (not word-by-word)
3. Uses proper voice intonation to give meaning
4. Has good posture and handles book appropriately
5. Understands simple punctuation:
   period (.)
   comma (,)
   question mark (?)
   exclamation mark (!)
B. Silent Reading
1. Reads without vocalization:
   Lip movements
   Whispering
2. Reads without head movements

Group Summary Profile—
First Level

The following pages present a Group Summary Profile at the First Level which you can use to record the progress of the entire class in mastering the specific reading skills at that level. This profile can assist you in identifying groups of students who need instruction in a particular skill as well as in assessing the strengths and achievement levels of individual students. The Group Profile may also be used in conferences with administrators to discuss the status of a particular class.

Name of Teacher: _____

GROUP SUMMARY
PROFILE
FIRST LEVEL

Student Names

I.	**Vocabulary:**
A.	**Word Recognition**
1.	Recognizes words with both upper and lower-case letters at beginning
2.	Knows names of letters in sequence
3.	Is able to identify in various settings words usually found in preprimers and primers
II.	**Word Analysis:**
A.	**Sound-symbol Association**
1.	Associates consonant sounds
2.	Names letter to represent consonant sounds
a.	Initial position
b.	Final position
c.	Medial position
3.	Discriminates between words
a.	Initial letter cues
b.	Final letter cues
4.	Associates sounds to digraphs
5.	Associates sounds to two letter blends
6.	Knows that the letters a, e, i, o, u, and combinations of these can represent several different sounds
B.	**Structural Analysis**
1.	Knows endings
a.	ed sound as "ed" in wanted
b.	ed sounds as "d" in moved
c.	ed sound as "t" in liked
2.	Recognizes compound words
3.	Knows common word families

(Blank grid for recording student data)

School: _____ Year: _____

C. **Word Form Clues**
1. Recognizes upper and lower-case letters
2. Recognizes words of different length
3. Recognizes words with double letters

III. **Comprehension**
A. Understands that printed symbols represent objects or actions
B. **Can follow printed directions**
C. **Can draw conclusions from given facts**
D. **Can recall from stories read aloud:**
1. Main idea
2. Names of characters
3. Important details
4. Stated sequence
E. **Can recall after silent reading:**
1. Main idea
2. Names of characters
3. Important details
4. Stated sequence
F. **Can distinguish between real and imaginary events**
G. **Uses context clues in word attack**
H. **Can suggest or select an appropriate title for a story**
I. **Can relate story content to own experiences**

IV. **Oral and Silent Reading Skills**
A. **Oral Reading**
1. Uses correct pronunciation
2. Uses correct phrasing (not word-by-word)
3. Uses proper voice intonation to give meaning
4. Has good posture and handles book appropriately
5. Understands simple punctuation:
   a. Period
   b. Comma
   c. Question mark
   d. Exclamation mark
B. **Silent Reading**
1. Reads without vocalization
2. Reads without head movements

Reading Skills Competency Tests First Level

Henriette L. Allen, Ph.D.
Wiley C. Thornton, M.Ed.

The test items which follow are written to measure the reading skills on the "Barbe Reading Skills Check List—First Level."

The Competency Tests and Check List provide for:

- a quick, informal assessment of a student's competence in reading skills
- diagnosis and prescription of specific reading skill weaknesses and needs
- devising of appropriate teaching strategies for individuals and small or large groups
- continuous evaluation of each student's progress in the basic reading skills
- flexibility in planning the reading instructional program
- immediate feedback to the student and the teacher

The tests are designed to give you an efficient, systematic means to identify the specific reading skills needs of students.

I.   VOCABULARY   A.   Word Recognition   1.   Upper- and lower-case letters at beginning

OBJECTIVE: The student will recognize a word as being the same whether it begins with an upper- or lower-case letter.

SAY: Look at the two words in each box. If the two words are not the same, make a mark through them. If they are the same, make no mark.

1. book
 	
    Book
	2. ~~Chin~~
	
	    ~~shin~~
		3. echo
		
		    Echo
			4. Sun
			
			    sun

5. quite
 	
    Quite
	6. ~~tray~~
	
	    ~~Gray~~
		7. ~~fine~~
		
		    ~~Line~~
			8. ~~Now~~
			
			    ~~how~~

MASTERY REQUIREMENT: All correct

Indicate mastery on the student response sheet with a check.

FIRST LEVEL

I. VOCABULARY

Name _____

Date _____

Mastery _____

A. Word Recognition

1. Upper- and lower-case letters at beginning

1. book Book	2. Chin shin	3. echo Echo	4. Sun sun
5. quite Quite	6. tray Gray	7. fine Line	8. Now how

I. VOCABULARY   A.   Word Recognition   2.   Names of letters in sequence

OBJECTIVE: The student will know the name of letters in sequence.

SAY: Look at this alphabet. Some of the letters have been left out. Read all of the letters aloud for me. When you come to a letter that has been left out, tell me what letter belongs there.

A   B   C   D   <u>E</u>   F   G   H   I   <u>J</u>   K   L   <u>M</u>

N   O   P   Q   <u>R</u>   S   T   U   <u>V</u>   W   X   <u>Y</u>   Z

MASTERY REQUIREMENT: All correct

Indicate mastery on the student response sheet with a check.

FIRST LEVEL

I. VOCABULARY

    A. Word Recognition

        2. Names of letters in sequence

A   B   C   D   _   F   G   H   I   _   K   L   _

N   O   P   Q   _   S   T   U   _   W   X   _   Z

FIRST LEVEL

I. VOCABULARY   A. Word Recognition   3. Words in preprimers and primers

OBJECTIVE: The student will identify words commonly found in preprimers and primers.

DIRECTIONS:

Option 1   Have the student say the words, noting on the student response sheet those words with which difficulty is encountered.

Option 2   Using flashcards, have the student say the words. Repeat the activity periodically until all the words have been mastered.

___ a	___ be	___ car	___ eat
___ about	___ bed	___ Christmas	___ farm
___ again	___ been	___ come	___ father
___ all	___ big	___ cookies	___ fast
___ am	___ birthday	___ could	___ find
___ an	___ black	___ cow	___ fine
___ and	___ blue	___ cowboy	___ fish
___ apple	___ boat	___ daddy	___ for
___ are	___ boy	___ day	___ from
___ as	___ but	___ did	___ fun
___ at	___ by	___ dinner	___ funny
___ away	___ cake	___ dish	___ get
___ baby	___ call	___ do	___ girl
___ back	___ came	___ dog	___ give
___ ball	___ can	___ down	___ go

MASTERY REQUIREMENT: Mastery of all the words by the end of the school year. (See additional words on pages 26 and 28.)

Indicate mastery on the student response sheet with a check.

24

FIRST LEVEL

I. VOCABULARY

A. Word Recognition

3. Words in preprimers and primers

Name _____

Date _____

Mastery _____

___ a	___ be	___ car	___ eat
___ about	___ bed	___ Christmas	___ farm
___ again	___ been	___ come	___ father
___ all	___ big	___ cookies	___ fast
___ am	___ birthday	___ could	___ find
___ an	___ black	___ cow	___ fine
___ and	___ blue	___ cowboy	___ fish
___ apple	___ boat	___ daddy	___ for
___ are	___ boy	___ day	___ from
___ as	___ but	___ did	___ fun
___ at	___ by	___ dinner	___ funny
___ away	___ cake	___ dish	___ get
___ baby	___ call	___ do	___ girl
___ back	___ came	___ dog	___ give
___ ball	___ can	___ down	___ go

FIRST LEVEL

I. VOCABULARY   **A.** Word Recognition   **3.** Words in preprimers and primers

OBJECTIVE: The student will identify words commonly found in preprimers and primers.

DIRECTIONS:

Option 1   Have the student say the words, noting on the student response sheet those words with which difficulty is encountered.

Option 2   Using flashcards, have the student say the words. Repeat the activity periodically until all the words have been mastered.

___ good	___ house	___ long	___ night
___ good-bye	___ how	___ look	___ no
___ green	___ I	___ make	___ not
___ has	___ if	___ man	___ of
___ had	___ in	___ many	___ on
___ happy	___ is	___ may	___ one
___ have	___ it	___ me	___ or
___ he	___ jump	___ mitten	___ party
___ help	___ just	___ mother	___ pie
___ her	___ kitten	___ more	___ play
___ here	___ know	___ morning	___ pretty
___ hide	___ laugh	___ must	___ puppy
___ him	___ let	___ my	___ put
___ his	___ like	___ near	___ rabbit
___ home	___ little	___ new	___ ran

MASTERY REQUIREMENT: Mastery of all the words by the end of the school year. (See additional words on pages 24 and 28.)

Indicate mastery on the student response sheet with a check.

FIRST LEVEL

I. **VOCABULARY**

    A. **Word Recognition**

        3. **Words in preprimers and primers**

Name _____

Date _____

Mastery _____

___ good	___ house	___ long	___ night
___ good-bye	___ how	___ look	___ no
___ green	___ I	___ make	___ not
___ has	___ if	___ man	___ of
___ had	___ in	___ many	___ on
___ happy	___ is	___ may	___ one
___ have	___ it	___ me	___ or
___ he	___ jump	___ mitten	___ party
___ help	___ just	___ mother	___ pie
___ her	___ kitten	___ more	___ play
___ here	___ know	___ morning	___ pretty
___ hide	___ laugh	___ must	___ puppy
___ him	___ let	___ my	___ put
___ his	___ like	___ near	___ rabbit
___ home	___ little	___ new	___ ran

I. VOCABULARY   A. Word Recognition   3. Words in preprimers and primers

OBJECTIVE: The student will be able to identify the words commonly found in preprimers and primers.

DIRECTIONS:

Option 1   Have the student say the words, noting on the student response sheet those words with which difficulty is encountered.

Option 2   Using flashcards, have the student say the words. Repeat the activity periodically until all the words have been mastered.

____red	___ stop	___ to	___ when
___ ride	___ surprise	___ too	___ where
___ run	___ TV	___ toy	___ which
___ said	___ table	___ two	___ white
___ sat	___ take	___ up	___ who
___ saw	___ thank	___ us	___ will
___ see	___ that	___ walk	___ wish
___ she	___ the	___ want	___ with
___ show	___ their	___ was	___ woman
___ sleep	___ them	___ water	___ work
___ so	___ then	___ way	___ would
___ some	___ there	___ we	___ yellow
___ something	___ they	___ went	___ yes
___ soon	___ this	___ were	___ you
___ splash	___ tree	___ what	___ your

MASTERY REQUIREMENT: Mastery of all the words by the end of the school year. (See additional words on page 24 and 26.)

Indicate mastery on the student response sheet with a check.

FIRST LEVEL

I. VOCABULARY

    A. Word Recognition

        3. Words in preprimers and primers

Name _____

Date _____

Mastery _____

___ red	___ stop	___ to	___ when
___ ride	___ surprise	___ too	___ where
___ run	___ TV	___ toy	___ which
___ said	___ table	___ two	___ white
___ sat	___ take	___ up	___ who
___ saw	___ thank	___ us	___ will
___ see	___ that	___ walk	___ wish
___ she	___ the	___ want	___ with
___ show	___ their	___ was	___ woman
___ sleep	___ them	___ water	___ work
___ so	___ then	___ way	___ would
___ some	___ there	___ we	___ yellow
___ something	___ they	___ went	___ yes
___ soon	___ this	___ were	___ you
___ splash	___ tree	___ what	___ your

II.   WORD ANALYSIS   A.   Sound-Symbol Associations   1.   Consonant sounds to letters

OBJECTIVE: The student will name and sound each single consonant.

DIRECTIONS: As the test is administered, use the student response sheet to check each letter.

SAY: As I point to the letters, tell me the name and the sound of the letter.

1. J _____   11. T _____

2. B _____   12. N _____

3. D _____   13. R _____

4. H _____   14. Y _____

5. L _____   15. M _____

6. F _____   16. Q _____

7. P _____   17. S _____

8. K _____   18. Z _____

9. V _____   19. W _____

10. L _____   20. X _____

MASTERY REQUIREMENT: 16 correct responses

Indicate mastery on the student response sheet with a check.

FIRST LEVEL

II. WORD ANALYSIS

A. Sound-Symbol Associations

1. Consonant sounds
   to letters

1. J _____

2. B _____

3. D _____

4. H _____

5. L _____

6. F _____

7. P _____

8. K _____

9. V _____

10. L _____

11. T _____

12. N _____

13. R _____

14. Y _____

15. M _____

16. Q _____

17. S _____

18. Z _____

19. W _____

20. X _____

II. WORD ANALYSIS   A. Sound-Symbol Associations   2. Names letters to represent consonant sounds heard

a. initial position

OBJECTIVE: The student will name letters which represent single consonant sounds heard at the beginning of words.

SAY: As I say these words, print the letter that names the first sound you hear in each of the words.

1. table   7. quart

2. zero   8. many

3. birthday   9. fish

4. house   10. party

5. yellow   11. work

6. little   12. run

MASTERY REQUIREMENT: 10 correct responses

Indicate mastery on the student response sheet with a check.

FIRST LEVEL

II. WORD ANALYSIS

    A. Sound-Symbol
        Associations

        2. Names letters to
            represent consonant
            sounds heard

            a. initial position

Name _____

Date _____

Mastery _____

1. _____

2. _____

3. _____

4. _____

5. _____

6. _____

7. _____

8. _____

9. _____

10. _____

11. _____

12. _____

II. WORD ANALYSIS   A. Sound-Symbol Associations   2. Names letters to represent consonant sounds heard

    b. final position

OBJECTIVE: The student will name letters which represent single consonant sounds heard at the end of words.

SAY: As I say these words, print the letter that names the last sound you hear in each of the words.

1. fee<u>t</u>   7. bo<u>x</u>

2. ra<u>n</u>   8. jo<u>b</u>

3. bu<u>zz</u>   9. roo<u>f</u>

4. ho<u>p</u>   10. di<u>d</u>

5. cal<u>l</u>   11. you<u>r</u>

6. ye<u>s</u>   12. hi<u>m</u>

MASTERY REQUIREMENT: 10 correct responses

Indicate mastery on the student response sheet with a check.

FIRST LEVEL

II. WORD ANALYSIS

    A. Sound-Symbol
        Associations

        2. Names letters to
            represent consonant
            sounds heard

            b. final position

Name _____

Date _____

Mastery _____

1. _____

2. _____

3. _____

4. _____

5. _____

6. _____

7. _____

8. _____

9. _____

10. _____

11. _____

12. _____

II.   WORD ANALYSIS   A.   Sound-Symbol Associations   2.   Names letters to
represent consonant
sounds heard

c.   medial position

OBJECTIVE: The student will name letters which represent single consonant sounds heard in
the medial position in words.

SAY: As I say these words, print the letter that names the sound you hear in the middle
of the word.

1. ma_ny   7. be_fore

2. sa_ving   8. far_mer

3. fu_nny   9. be_yond

4. pi_llow   10. to_day

5. se_ven   11. hi_tting

6. pu_ppy   12. unh_appy

MASTERY REQUIREMENT: 10 correct responses

Indicate mastery on the student response sheet with a check.

II.   WORD ANALYSIS   Name _____

    A.   Sound-Symbol
        Associations   Date _____

        2.   Names letters to
            represent consonant   Mastery _____
            sounds heard

            c.   medial position

                1. _____   7. _____

                2. _____   8. _____

                3. _____   9. _____

                4. _____   10. _____

                5. _____   11. _____

                6. _____   12. _____

FIRST LEVEL

II. WORD ANALYSIS   A. Sound-Symbol Associations   3. Discriminates between words

a. initial letter cues

OBJECTIVE: The student will discriminate between words which are similar using the initial letter as a cue.

SAY: Look at the words that are side by side on your paper. Listen carefully as I say one word from each of the pairs, then you draw a circle around the word I say.

DIRECTIONS: Say the circled word of the pair.

1. hoof   (roof)

2. (hat)   sat

3. spoon   (soon)

4. ring   (sing)

5. pick   (kick)

6. (goat)   boat

7. (must)   rust

8. latch   (catch)

MASTERY REQUIREMENT: 7 correct responses

Indicate mastery on the student response sheet with a check.

FIRST LEVEL

II. WORD ANALYSIS

    A. Sound-Symbol
        Associations

       3. Discriminates between
           words

          a. initial letter cues

Name _____

Date _____

Mastery _____

1. hoof   roof

2. hat   sat

3. spoon   soon

4. ring   sing

5. pick   kick

6. goat   boat

7. must   rush

8. latch   catch

II.   WORD ANALYSIS   A.   Sound-Symbol Associations   3.   Discriminates between words

b.   final letter cues

OBJECTIVE: The student will discriminate between words which are similar using the final letter as a cue.

SAY: Look at the words that are side by side on your paper. Listen carefully as I say one word from each of the pairs, then you draw a circle around the word I say.

DIRECTIONS: Say the circled word of the pair.

1. cook   (cool)

2. (bear)   boat

3. (half)   halt

4. tail   (train)

5. fine   (find)

6. been   (beat)

7. (wood)   wool

8. help   (held)

MASTERY REQUIREMENT: 7 correct responses

Indicate mastery on the student response sheet with a check.

II.   WORD ANALYSIS

    A.   Sound-Symbol
        Associations

        3.   Discriminates between
            words

            b.   final letter cues

Name _____

Date _____

Mastery _____

1.   cook   cool

2.   bear   boat

3.   half   halt

4.   tail   train

5.   fine   find

6.   been   beat

7.   wood   wool

8.   help   held

II. WORD ANALYSIS   A. Sound-Symbol Associations   4. Association of sounds to
                                                                  digraphs

OBJECTIVE: The student will associate the sounds to the digraphs sh, wh, th, and ch.

SAY: Look at these words. In each pair, draw a circle around the word that I say.

DIRECTIONS: Say the circled word.

1. (where)   were

2. tin   (thin)

3. sell   (shell)

4. (chin)   fin

5. (this)   miss

6. girl   (whirl)

7. (church)   knock

8. seventy   (seventh)

MASTERY REQUIREMENT: 7 correct responses

Indicate mastery on the student response sheet with a check.

II. WORD ANALYSIS

Name _____

   A.   Sound-Symbol
        Associations

Date _____

      4.   Association of sounds
           to digraphs

Mastery _____

   1.   where   were

   2.   tin   thin

   3.   sell   shell

   4.   chin   fin

   5.   this   miss

   6.   girl   whirl

   7.   church   knock

   8.   seventy   seventh

II.   WORD ANALYSIS   A.   Sound-Symbol Associations   5.   Associates sounds to
                                                                     two-letter blends

OBJECTIVE: The student will associate sounds to two-letter blends.

SAY: Here are some words with the first two letters missing. For each word I say, you
             print the first two letters in the blanks.

1.   stand   9.   grape

2.   blue   10. spin

3.   please   11. smile

4.   train   12. snap

5.   from   13. swim

6.   fly   14. bring

7.   clear   15. grow

8.   glass   16. slip

MASTERY REQUIREMENT: 14 correct responses

Indicate mastery on the student response sheet with a check.

II.   WORD ANALYSIS

    A.   Sound-Symbol
         Associations

         5.   Associates sounds to
             two-letter blends

Name _____

Date _____

Mastery _____

1.   __ __ and

2.   __ __ ue

3.   __ __ ease

4.   __ __ ain

5.   __ __ om

6.   __ __ y

7.   __ __ ear

8.   __ __ ass

9.   __ __ ape

10.   __ __ in

11.   __ __ ile

12.   __ __ ap

13.   __ __ im

14.   __ __ ing

15.   __ __ ow

16.   __ __ ip

II. WORD ANALYSIS   A.   Sound-Symbol Associations   6.   Vowel sounds

OBJECTIVE: The student will know the letters a, e, i, o, and u and combinations of these can represent several different sounds.

SAY: Look at all the words after No. 1 on your paper. Draw a circle around each word that has the same "a" sound you hear in "cake."

1.   (make)   sat   (late)   cat   (pay)   (maid)   (lake)   (grade)

Look at all the words after No. 2 on your paper. Draw a circle around each word that has the same "e" sound you hear in "pet."

2.   (get)   see   we   (less)   bean   easy   (bed)   bead

Look at all the words after No. 3 on your paper. Draw a circle around each word that has the same "i" sound you hear in "nice."

3.   (rice)   bit   (bike)   (write)   tin   (right)   trip   (life)

Look at all the words after No. 4 on your paper. Draw a circle around each word that has the same "o" sound you hear in "mop."

4.   mope   (top)   sound   (Bob)   do   log   soap   (sob)

Look at all the words after No. 5 on your paper. Draw a circle around each word that has the same "u" sound you hear in "tub."

5.   rule   (rub)   (puppy)   due   (but)   (gull)   (grub)   suit

MASTERY REQUIREMENT: 18 correct responses

Indicate mastery on the student response sheet with a check.

FIRST LEVEL

II. WORD ANALYSIS

    A. Sound-Symbol
          Associations

        6. Vowel sounds

Name _____

Date _____

Mastery _____

1. make   sat   late   cat   pay   maid   lake   grade

2. get   see   we   less   bean   easy   bed   bead

3. rice   bit   bike   write   tin   right   trip   life

4. mope   top   sound   Bob   do   log   soap   sob

5. rule   rub   puppy   due   but   gull   grub   suit

II. WORD ANALYSIS   B. Structural Analysis   1. Endings   a. ed sound as "ed"

OBJECTIVE: The student will identify words in which the ed ending makes the "ed" sound.

SAY: Look at the words on your paper as I read them. If you hear the "ed" sound at the end of the word, circle the "yes" beside the word. If you do not, circle the "no."

1. waited   (yes)   no

2. wanted   (yes)   no

3. rained   yes   (no)

4. added   (yes)   no

5. crossed   yes   (no)

MASTERY REQUIREMENT: 4 correct responses

Indicate mastery on the student response sheet with a check.

FIRST LEVEL

II. WORD ANALYSIS

    B. Structural Analysis

        1. Endings

            a. ed sound as "ed"

Name _____

Date _____

Mastery _____

1. waited   yes   no

2. wanted   yes   no

3. rained   yes   no

4. added   yes   no

5. crossed   yes   no

II. WORD ANALYSIS   B. Structural Analysis   1. Endings   b. ed sound as "d"

OBJECTIVE: The student will identify words in which the ed ending makes the "d" sound.

SAY: Look at the words on your paper as I read them. If you hear the "d" sound at the end of the word, circle the "yes" beside the word. If you do not, circle the "no."

1. filled   (yes)   no

2. curled   (yes)   no

3. gained   (yes)   no

4. dented   yes   (no)

5. checked   yes   (no)

MASTERY REQUIREMENT: 4 correct responses

Indicate mastery on the student response sheet with a check.

FIRST LEVEL

II.   WORD ANALYSIS

    B.   Structural Analysis

        1.   Endings

            b.   ed sound as "d"

Name _____

Date _____

Mastery _____

1.   filled   yes   no

2.   curled   yes   no

3.   gained   yes   no

4.   dented   yes   no

5.   checked   yes   no

FIRST LEVEL

II.   WORD ANALYSIS   B.   Structural Analysis   1.   Endings   c.   ed sound as "t"

OBJECTIVE: The student will identify words in which the ed ending makes the "t" sound.

SAY: Look at the words on your paper as I read them. If you hear the "t" sound at the end of the word, circle the "yes" beside the word. If you do not, circle the "no."

1.   backed   (yes)   no

2.   lasted   yes   (no)

3.   fixed   (yes)   no

4.   bluffed   (yes)   no

5.   purred   yes   (no)

MASTERY REQUIREMENT: 4 correct responses

Indicate mastery on the student response sheet with a check.

II.   WORD ANALYSIS   Name _____

    B.   **Structural Analysis**

        1.   **Endings**   Date _____

           c.   ed sound as "t"   Mastery _____

1.   backed   yes   no

2.   lasted   yes   no

3.   fixed   yes   no

4.   bluffed   yes   no

5.   purred   yes   no

II. WORD ANALYSIS   B. Structural Analysis   2. Compound words

OBJECTIVE: The student will recognize compound words.

SAY:

Option 1   Look at this list of words. Circle each word that is a compound word.

Option 2   Listen to these words and tell me which ones are compound words.

1. (baseball)

2. surprise

3. walked

4. (upon)

5. table

6. farmer

7. chair

8. (cowboy)

9. (into)

10. against

11. (playmate)

MASTERY REQUIREMENT: No errors

Indicate mastery on the student response sheet with a check.

FIRST LEVEL

II. WORD ANALYSIS

    B.   Structural Analysis

        2.   Compound words

Name _____

Date _____

Mastery _____

1. baseball

2. surprise

3. walked

4. upon

5. table

6. farmer

7. chair

8. cowboy

9. into

10. against

11. playmate

II. WORD ANALYSIS   B. Structural Analysis   3. Word families

OBJECTIVE: The student will demonstrate knowledge of common word families.

SAY: Print one or more letters on the line that can go with the letters that are already there to make different words. Look at No. 1. By adding letters at the beginning, you could make <u>b</u>all, <u>c</u>all, <u>sm</u>all, <u>h</u>all, <u>f</u>all.

1.

    <u>f</u> all

    <u>c</u> all

    <u>t</u> all

2.

    <u>s</u> at

    <u>m</u> at

    <u>p</u> at

3.

    <u>l</u> it

    <u>b</u> it

    <u>s</u> it

4.

    <u>c</u> an

    <u>p</u> an

    <u>r</u> an

5.

    <u>p</u> ill

    <u>st</u> ill

    <u>w</u> ill

6.

    <u>p</u> et

    <u>j</u> et

    <u>l</u> et

7.

    <u>s</u> ell

    <u>sh</u> ell

    <u>t</u> ell

8.

    <u>p</u> ay

    <u>m</u> ay

    <u>pl</u> ay

9.

    <u>s</u> ake

    <u>b</u> ake

    <u>l</u> ake

DIRECTIONS: Many responses are acceptable in addition to those given. (See additional word families covered on page 58.)

MASTERY REQUIREMENT: 7 correct responses

Indicate mastery on the student response sheet with a check.

II. WORD ANALYSIS

    B. Structural Analysis

       3. Word families

Name _____

Date _____

Mastery _____

1. _____ all   2. _____ at   3. _____ it

    _____ all   _____ at   _____ it

    _____ all   _____ at   _____ it

---

4. _____ an   5. _____ ill   6. _____ et

    _____ an   _____ ill   _____ et

    _____ an   _____ ill   _____ et

---

7. _____ ell   8. _____ ay   9. _____ ake

    _____ ell   _____ ay   _____ ake

    _____ ell   _____ ay   _____ ake

II. WORD ANALYSIS   B.   Structural Analysis   3.   Word families

OBJECTIVE: The student will demonstrate knowledge of common word families.

SAY: Print one or more letters on the line that can go with the letters that are already there to make different words. Look at No. 1. By adding letters at the beginning, you could make <u>b</u>all, <u>c</u>all, <u>sm</u>all, <u>h</u>all, <u>f</u>all.

1.

<u> w </u> all

<u> f </u> all

<u> h </u> all

2.

<u> b </u> ook

<u> c </u> ook

<u> br </u> ook

3.

<u> br </u> ing

<u> s </u> ing

<u> r </u> ing

4.

<u> s </u> ack

<u> b </u> ack

<u> t </u> ack

5.

<u> w </u> in

<u> p </u> in

<u> t </u> in

6.

<u> w </u> ish

<u> f </u> ish

<u> d </u> ish

7.

<u> l </u> ight

<u> s </u> ight

<u> br </u> ight

8.

<u> f </u> ill

<u> s </u> ill

<u> b </u> ill

9.

<u> b </u> et

<u> s </u> et

<u> m </u> et

DIRECTIONS: Many responses are acceptable in addition to those given. (See additional word families covered on page 56.)

MASTERY REQUIREMENT: 7 correct responses

Indicate mastery on the student response sheet with a check.

II. WORD ANALYSIS

Name _____

B. Structural Analysis

3. Word families

Date _____

Mastery _____

1. _____ all   2. _____ ook   3. _____ ing

   _____ all   _____ ook   _____ ing

   _____ all   _____ ook   _____ ing

4. _____ ack   5. _____ in   6. _____ ish

   _____ ack   _____ in   _____ ish

   _____ ack   _____ in   _____ ish

7. _____ ight   8. _____ ill   9. _____ et

   _____ ight   _____ ill   _____ et

   _____ ight   _____ ill   _____ et

II.   WORD ANALYSIS   C.   Word Form Clues   1.   Recognition of upper- and lower-case letters

OBJECTIVE: The student will recognize upper- and lower-case letters.

SAY: Draw a circle around the upper-case or capital letters.

(A)	a	n	(N)
b	(B)	o	(O)
c	(C)	(P)	p
d	(D)	(Q)	q
(E)	e	r	(R)
f	(F)	s	(S)
(G)	g	(T)	t
(H)	h	(U)	u
(I)	i	(V)	v
j	(J)	w	(W)
(K)	k	x	(X)
l	(L)	(Y)	y
(M)	m	(Z)	z

MASTERY REQUIREMENT: All correct

Indicate mastery on the student response sheet with a check.

FIRST LEVEL

II. WORD ANALYSIS

    C. Word Form Clues

        1. Recognition of upper- and
            lower-case letters

Name _____

Date _____

Mastery _____

A	a		K	k		U	u
b	B		l	L		V	v
c	C		M	m		w	W
d	D		n	N		x	X
E	e		o	O		Y	y
f	F		P	p		Z	z
G	g		Q	q			
H	h		r	R			
I	i		s	S			
j	J		T	t			

II.   WORD ANALYSIS   C.   Word Form Clues   2.   Length of word

OBJECTIVE: The student recognizes that length of words may give a clue to their identification.

SAY: Listen as I say some pairs of words. As I say each pair, if you think the first word is longer, draw a circle around the "1" on your paper. If you think the second word is longer, draw a circle around the "2."

a. day	ladder	1	(2)
b. window	door	(1)	2
c. September	June	(1)	2
d. wall	ceiling	1	(2)
e. pine	pineapple	1	(2)
f. remember	real	(1)	2
g. today	tomorrow	1	(2)
h. accordion	ant	(1)	2
i. tennis	Tennessee	1	(2)
j. famous	fact	(1)	2

MASTERY REQUIREMENT: 8 correct responses

Indicate mastery on the student response sheet with a check.

FIRST LEVEL

II.   WORD ANALYSIS

    C.   Word Form Clues

        2.   Length of word

Name _____

Date _____

Mastery _____

a.   1   2

b.   1   2

c.   1   2

d.   1   2

e.   1   2

f.   1   2

g.   1   2

h.   1   2

i.   1   2

j.   1   2

II. WORD ANALYSIS   C. Word Form Clues   3. Double letters

OBJECTIVE: The student recognizes words which have double letters.

SAY: In each of the following, draw a circle around the word which has double letters.

1. (apple)   ant

2. the   (tree)

3. let   (look)

4. bat   (ball)

5. (funny)   four

6. (mitten)   mouse

7. slap   (sleep)

8. (little)   like

9. yesterday   (yellow)

10. (happy)   hunting

MASTERY REQUIREMENT: 8 correct responses

Indicate mastery on the student response sheet with a check.

II. WORD ANALYSIS

    C. Word Form Clues

        3. Double letters

Name _____

Date _____

Mastery _____

1.	apple	ant
2.	the	tree
3.	let	look
4.	bat	ball
5.	funny	four
6.	mitten	mouse
7.	slap	sleep
8.	little	like
9.	yesterday	yellow
10.	happy	hunting

III.   COMPREHENSION   A.   Symbolic Representation

OBJECTIVE: The student identifies printed symbols representing objects or actions.

DIRECTIONS: Make a check mark in the blank by each picture or symbol on the student response sheet which the pupil is able to discuss demonstrating understanding.

SAY: Talk with me about all the things you see on this page.

1. _____

2. _____

3. _____

4. _____

5. _____

6. _____

7. _____

8. _____

9. _____

MASTERY REQUIREMENT: 6 responses judged to be adequate.

Indicate mastery on the student response sheet with a check.

FIRST LEVEL

III. COMPREHENSION

    A. Symbolic Representation

Name _____

Date _____

Mastery _____

1. _____

2. _____

3. _____

4. _____

5. _____

6. _____

7. _____

8. _____

9. _____

III. COMPREHENSION   B.   Following Printed Directions

OBJECTIVE: The student will demonstrate the ability to follow simple printed directions.

SAY: Look at each of these pictures. Read what is said next to the picture and do what the directions say.

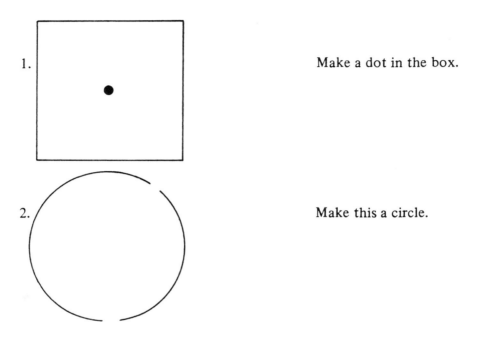

Make a dot in the box.

Make this a circle.

3. _____ (student's name) _____   Print your name on the line.

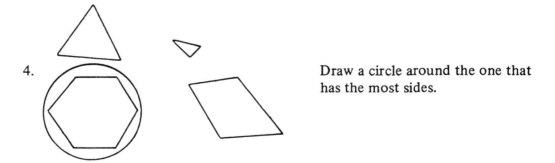

Draw a circle around the one that has the most sides.

MASTERY REQUIREMENT: 3 correct responses

Indicate mastery on the student response sheet with a check.

FIRST LEVEL

III. COMPREHENSION

    B. Following Printed
        Directions

Name _____

Date _____

Mastery _____

1.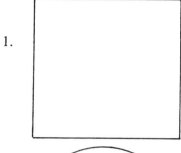

Make a dot in the box.

2.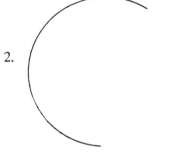

Make this a circle.

3.

Print your name on the line.

4.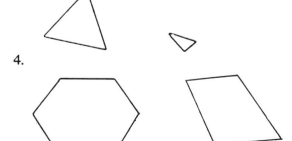

Draw a circle around the one
that has the most sides.

FIRST LEVEL

III.   COMPREHENSION   C.   Drawing Conclusions

OBJECTIVE: The student will draw conclusions from given facts.

SAY: Listen carefully as I read you a short story.

"This has been a terrible day," said Sue. "The car wouldn't start this morning. Then I dropped the box I was carrying. And besides that, I broke the band on my new watch this afternoon."

Now look at the three sentences that are above the line on your paper.

_____   1.   Sue was silly.

  X   2.   Sue was not happy.

_____   3.   Sue was sick with a cold.

Put an X by the sentence that tells how Sue feels.

Now listen to another story.

Jim was walking through the woods when he saw what he thought was a piece of rope across the path in front of him. He wondered what a piece of rope was doing out there in the woods. A few steps away, he stopped to look. Just then the piece of rope moved. One end started to lift up off the ground and Jim heard a rattling noise.

Look at the three sentences that are below the line on your paper.

_____   1.   Jim should get closer to see what is happening.

_____   2.   Jim should try to grab it to stop it from moving.

  X   3.   Jim should move quickly away from there.

Put an X by the sentence that tells what Jim should do.

MASTERY REQUIREMENT: Both correct

Indicate mastery on the student response sheet with a check.

III.   COMPREHENSION

    C.   Drawing Conclusions

Name _____

Date _____

Mastery _____

_____ 1.   Sue was silly.

_____ 2.   Sue was not happy.

_____ 3.   Sue was sick with a cold.

_____

_____ 1.   Jim should get closer to see what is happening.

_____ 2.   Jim should try to grab it to stop it from moving.

_____ 3.   Jim should move quickly away from there.

III.   COMPREHENSION   D.   Recall from Stories Read Aloud   1. Main idea

OBJECTIVE: From a story read aloud, the student will select the main idea of the story.

DIRECTIONS: Have the student read the story aloud. Give assistance on any words with which difficulty is encountered.

BY STUDENT: When I am sick, I can help other children keep from getting sick. I should remember not to sneeze or cough in other children's faces when I have a cold. I should always use my handkerchief to cover my mouth when I cough. Even when I am just talking to others, I should not put my face very close to theirs. I should never put my mouth on the water fountain, because this may spread my germs to someone else.

SAY: Now look at the sentences below. Make an X by the one that tells the main idea of what you read.

_____   a.   This story told how to use a water fountain.

_X_   b.   This story was about how to keep from spreading cold germs.

_____   c.   This story was about having a cold.

MASTERY REQUIREMENT: Correct response

Indicate mastery on the student response sheet with a check.

III. COMPREHENSION

D. Recall from Stories
    Read Aloud

    1. Main idea

Name _____

Date _____

Mastery _____

When I am sick, I can help other children keep from getting sick. I should remember not to sneeze or cough in other children's faces when I have a cold. I should always use my handkerchief to cover my mouth when I cough. Even when I am just talking to others, I should not put my face very close to theirs. I should never put my mouth on the water fountain, because this may spread my germs to someone else.

_____ a. This story told how to use a water fountain.

_____ b. This story was about how to keep from spreading cold germs.

_____ c. This story was about having a cold.

III. COMPREHENSION   D.   Recall from Stories Read Aloud   2.   Names of characters

OBJECTIVE: From a story read aloud, the student will recall the names of characters.

DIRECTIONS: Have the student read the story aloud. Give assistance on any words with which difficulty is encountered.

SAY: Read this story aloud to me then give me your paper and I will ask you some questions about the story.

BY STUDENT: Jan West was a city girl. She and her parents, Mr. and Mrs. West, lived in a big building called an apartment house. No large pets like dogs or cats were allowed to live in the apartment house, so Jan had a parrot named Mike for a pet.

Tim Ross was Jan's cousin. Tim did not live in the city. He lived on a farm. Tim's family owned many animals. Tim had two dogs and three cats for pets, but there were many more animals on the farm, such as chickens, horses, cows, and sheep. None of the farm animals had names like pets do except for the big red rooster that woke them up crowing every morning. They named him Sunrise!

DIRECTIONS: Record answers to questions on student response sheet.

SAY:
1. The last name of the girl in the story was West. What was her first name?

      Jan

2. Who was Mike?   a parrot

3. The boy's name in the story was   Tim   .

4. What was the rooster's name?   Sunrise

MASTERY REQUIREMENT: 3 correct responses

Indicate mastery on the student response sheet with a check.

III. COMPREHENSION

Name _____

D. Recall from Stories
Read Aloud

Date _____

2. Names of characters

Mastery _____

Jan West was a city girl. She and her parents, Mr. and Mrs. West, lived in a big building called an apartment house. No large pets like dogs or cats were allowed to live in the apartment house, so Jan had a parrot named Mike for a pet.

Tim Ross was Jan's cousin. Tim did not live in the city. He lived on a farm. Tim's family owned many animals. Tim had two dogs and three cats for pets, but there were many more animals on the farm, such as chickens, horses, cows, and sheep. None of the farm animals had names like pets do except for the big red rooster that woke them up crowing every morning. They named him Sunrise!

1. _____

2. _____

3. _____

4. _____

III.   COMPREHENSION   D.   Recall from Stories Read Aloud   3.   Details

OBJECTIVE: From a story read aloud, the student will recall details.

DIRECTIONS: Have the student read the story aloud. Give assistance on any words with which difficulty is encountered.

SAY: Read this story aloud to me, then give me your paper and I will ask you some questions about the story.

BY STUDENT: Sandy was tired. He had helped his mother all morning. After breakfast, he had washed the dishes and put them away. While his mother cleaned the rugs, Sandy dusted all the furniture. When they finished cleaning in the house, they went outside and pulled the weeds from the flower beds. Now it was time to eat lunch. Just as they began to eat, the phone rang. It was Dad. He said, "Since you two have been sitting around resting all morning, let's all go to the zoo when I get home from work."

DIRECTIONS: Read the following questions and responses to the student. Check response given by student on student response sheet.

SAY: Now answer these questions for me.

1.   What did Sandy do while his mother cleaned rugs?

    _____   a.   Rested.
    _ x _   b.   Dusted.
    _____   c.   Pulled weeds.

2.   Who washed the dishes after breakfast?

    _____   a.   Mother.
    _____   b.   Father.
    _ x _   c.   Sandy.

3.   When did Dad call?

    _____   a.   After lunch.
    _____   b.   While they were weeding flowers.
    _ x _   c.   While they were eating lunch.

MASTERY REQUIREMENT: All correct

Indicate mastery on the student response sheet with a check.

III. COMPREHENSION

D. Recall from Stories
Read Aloud

3. Details

Name _____

Date _____

Mastery _____

Sandy was tired. He had helped his mother all morning. After breakfast, he had washed the dishes and put them away. While his mother cleaned the rugs, Sandy dusted all the furniture. When they finished cleaning in the house, they went outside and pulled the weeds from the flower beds. Now it was time to eat lunch. Just as they began to eat, the phone rang. It was Dad. He said, "Since you two have been sitting around resting all morning, let's all go to the zoo when I get home from work."

1. _____ a.   2. _____ a.   3. _____ a.

_____ b.   _____ b.   _____ b.

_____ c.   _____ c.   _____ c.

III.   COMPREHENSION   D.   Recall from Stories Read Aloud   4.   Stated sequence

OBJECTIVE: From a story read aloud, the student will place events in stated sequence.

DIRECTIONS: Have the student read the story aloud. Give assistance on any words with which difficulty is encountered.

SAY: Read this story aloud to me, then give me your paper and I will ask you some questions about the story.

BY STUDENT: A big jay scolding outside her window woke Jennifer up early one morning. It was too early to get up, but she decided to stay awake and listen to everything outside. She heard a truck stop in front of the house. "Who could that be?" she wondered. Then she heard bottles rattling and knew it was the milkman bringing their milk. Soon she heard a car stop next door and someone go in that house. "That must be Mr. Todd," Jennifer thought. "He works at night, so he gets home and goes to bed just as most people are getting up." After that, Jennifer must have gone back to sleep, because the next thing she knew, Mother was calling her to get ready for breakfast.

DIRECTIONS: After obtaining student response sheet, read the following:

SAY: I am going to read four things that happened in the story, but they will not be in the right order. You are to listen, then try to remember the order they really happened in the story.

KEY:

a.   The milk came.   2

b.   The jay woke Jennifer up.   1

c.   Jennifer's mother called.   4

d.   Mr. Todd came home from work.   3

DIRECTIONS: Record responses on student response sheet. It is permissible to repeat the items as necessary.

MASTERY REQUIREMENT: All correct

Indicate mastery on the student response sheet with a check.

III. COMPREHENSION

D. Recall from Stories
    Read Aloud

4. Stated sequence

Name _____

Date _____

Mastery _____

A big jay scolding outside her window woke Jennifer up early one morning. It was too early to get up, but she decided to stay awake and listen to everything outside. She heard a truck stop in front of the house. "Who could that be?" she wondered. Then she heard bottles rattling and knew it was the milkman bringing their milk. Soon she heard a car stop next door and someone go in that house. "That must be Mr. Todd," Jennifer thought. "He works at night, so he gets home and goes to bed just as most people are getting up." After that, Jennifer must have gone back to sleep, because the next thing she knew, Mother was calling her to get ready for breakfast.

1. _____

2. _____

3. _____

4. _____

III.   COMPREHENSION   E.   Recall after Silent Reading   1.   Main idea

OBJECTIVE: The student will recall the main idea of a story after reading it silently.

DIRECTIONS: Have the student read the story silently and fill in the correct answers.

SAY: Read this to yourself. When you have finished, fill in the blanks at the bottom.

> Are there stars in the sky at night?
> Yes.
> Are there stars in the sky in the daytime?
> Yes. There are just as many stars in daytime as there are at night.
> Do you know why we can't see them during the daytime?
> We can't see them because the sun makes the sky too bright.
> At night when the sky is dark, the stars look bright. But in the daytime when the sky is brighter than the stars, we can't see the stars.
> But they are still there and they are still shining.

1.   Do the stars stop shining in daytime?   no

2.   In the daytime the sun (or sky) is so bright it keeps us from seeing the stars.

MASTERY REQUIREMENT: Both correct

Indicate mastery on the student response sheet with a check.

III. COMPREHENSION

Name _____

E. Recall after Silent
Reading

Date _____

1. Main idea

Mastery _____

Are there stars in the sky at night?

Yes.

Are there stars in the sky in the daytime?

Yes. There are just as many stars in daytime as there are at night.

Do you know why we can't see them during the daytime? We can't see them because the sun makes the sky too bright.

At night when the sky is dark, the stars look bright. But in the daytime when the sky is brighter than the stars, we can't see the stars.

But they are still there and they are still shining.

1. Do the stars stop shining in daytime? _____

2. In the daytime the _____ is so bright it keeps us from seeing the stars.

III. COMPREHENSION   E.   Recall after Silent Reading   2.   Names of characters

OBJECTIVE: After reading a story silently, the student will recall the names of the characters in the story.

SAY: Read this story to yourself and then I am going to ask you some questions about it.

> Carol and Marie Bear were twins. They lived on Maple Street.
> David and Danny Deer were also twins. They lived on Oak Street.
> Carol and Marie did not know David and Danny before school started.
> Both pairs of twins were excited to learn that they were in the same grade.
> They had never thought they would have twins for best friends.
> Why, they both even lived on a street named after a tree!

SAY: In the blanks near the bottom of your paper, print the answer to these questions. Try to answer the questions without looking back.

1.   What was Carol's sister's name?   Marie

2.   What was Danny's brother's name?   David

3.   Both street names were trees. The last name of
     both sets of twins were the names of animals.
     What were they?   Deer

                                                        Bear

MASTERY REQUIREMENT: 3 correct responses

Indicate mastery on the student response sheet with a check.

III. COMPREHENSION

    E. Recall after Silent
       Reading

       2. Names of characters

Name _____

Date _____

Mastery _____

Carol and Marie Bear were twins.

They lived on Maple Street.

David and Danny Deer were also twins.

They lived on Oak Street.

Carol and Marie did not know David and Danny before school started.

Both pairs of twins were excited to learn that they were in the same grade.

They had never thought they would have twins for best friends.

Why, they both even lived on a street named after a tree!

1. _____

2. _____

3. _____

4. _____

III. COMPREHENSION   E. Recall after Silent Reading   3. Important details

OBJECTIVE: After reading a story silently, the student will recall important details from the story.

SAY: Read this story to yourself and then I am going to ask you some questions about it.

Mother said, "I heard there is a circus in town. I will take you to the circus this afternoon. How would you like that?"

"Oh, that will be fun," Barb cried.

"Yes," said Ellen, "I love to watch the clowns. They are so funny!"

"I like them too," said Barb, "but I think I like the elephants best. How do they ever teach them to do the tricks they do?"

Mother said, "I like all those things too, but what I really like to see is the way people in the trapeze act fly through the air so high on the swings and ropes and catch each other. How they must work and practice to learn to do those tricks without falling!"

SAY: In the blanks near the bottom of your paper, print the answer to these questions. You may look back at the story if you have difficulty. However, try to answer the questions without looking back. Select your answers from the group of words given.

1. Where did Mother say she would take them when they finished?   ___circus___

2. In which animal was Barb especially interested?   ___elephant___

3. What did Ellen look forward to seeing?   ___clowns___

4. What did Mother like to see?   ___trapeze act___

MASTERY REQUIREMENT: 3 correct responses.

Indicate mastery on the student sheet with a check.

III. COMPREHENSION

    E.   **Recall after Silent Reading**

        3. **Important details**

Name _____

Date _____

Mastery _____

Mother said, "I heard there is a circus in town. I will take you to the circus this afternoon. How would you like that?"

"Oh, that will be fun," Barb cried.

"Yes," said Ellen, "I love to watch the clowns. They are so silly!"

"I like them too," said Barb, "but I think I like the elephants best. How do they ever teach them to do the tricks they do."

Mother said, "I like all those things too, but what I really like to see is the way people in the trapeze act fly through the air so high on the swings and ropes and catch each other. How they must work and practice to learn to do those tricks without falling!"

1. _____   elephant

2. _____   practice

3. _____   trapeze act

4. _____   clowns

                                              circus

III. COMPREHENSION   E. Recall after Silent Reading   4. Stated sequence

OBJECTIVE: After reading a story silently, the student will recall the sequence of important events in the story.

SAY: Read this to yourself and then I am going to ask you some questions about it.

Mark got a cloth and washed his hands. He brushed his teeth, then put on clean clothes.
Then he combed his hair.

SAY: Try to answer these questions without looking back at what you read.

By No. 1 on your paper, make an X by the last thing the story said Mark did.

_____ a.   got a cloth

__X__ b.   combed his hair

_____ c.   shined his shoes

2.   After he washed his hands, what did he do next?

_____ a.   combed his hair

_____ b.   got a cloth

__X__ c.   brushed his teeth

3.   What was the first thing Mark did?

__X__ a.   got a cloth

_____ b.   brushed his teeth

_____ c.   changed his socks

MASTERY REQUIREMENT: 2 correct responses

Indicate mastery on the student response sheet with a check.

III. COMPREHENSION

Name _____

    E.   Recall after Silent
        Reading

Date _____

        4.   Stated sequence

Mastery _____

Mark got a cloth and washed his hands. He brushed his teeth, then put on clean clothes.
Then he combed his hair.

1. _____ a. got a cloth

   _____ b. combed his hair

   _____ c. shined his shoes

2. _____ a. combed his hair

   _____ b. got a cloth

   _____ c. brushed his teeth

3. _____ a. got a cloth

   _____ b. brushed his teeth

   _____ c. changed his socks

III.   COMPREHENSION   F.   Distinguish Real from Imaginary

OBJECTIVE: The student will identify statements as real or imaginary.

SAY: I am going to read you some sentences that are parts of stories. Some of these statements will be about things that are real or could really happen; and some of them will be about things or will say things that could not be real. After I read each sentence, mark your paper by drawing a circle around "could be real" or "could not be real."

1.   Suddenly the dark clouds moved across the sky and we heard thunder.

   (Could be real)   Could not be real

2.   "I think I can, I think I can," puffed the little locomotive as it pulled the long line of freight cars up the steep hill.

   Could be real   (Could not be real)

3.   "Why do you wear those silly striped pajamas all the time?" the little monkey asked the zebra.

   Could be real   (Could not be real)

4.   "Come quickly and look! Judy bought a new car. Look how bright and shiny it is!" cried Tommy.

   (Could be real)   Could not be real

5.   The little boat almost overturned as the huge waves crashed against it.

   (Could be real)   Could not be real

6.   Alice found that every time she put an oak leaf into the magic red box, it turned into a crisp, new dollar.

   Could be real   (Could not be real)

MASTERY REQUIREMENT: 5 correct response

Indicate mastery on the student response sheet with a check.

FIRST LEVEL

III. COMPREHENSION

    F. Distinguishing Real from
        Imaginary

Name _____

Date _____

Mastery _____

1.   Could be real   Could not be real

2.   Could be real   Could not be real

3.   Could be real   Could not be real

4.   Could be real   Could not be real

5.   Could be real   Could not be real

6.   Could be real   Could not be real

III. COMPREHENSION   G.   Context Clues

OBJECTIVE: The student will demonstrate use of context clues in word attack.

SAY: Read the following sentences to yourself as I read them aloud. After each sentence, I'll give you a little time to think of a good word to go in the blank. After you think of a word, print it in the blank.

1.   When you go out, please close the ____(door)____ quietly.

2.   After we eat, we should always brush our ____(teeth)____ .

3.   I am going to bake a big chocolate ____(cake)____ for dessert.

4.   The kitten climbed up to the top of the big pine ____(tree)____ .

5.   I lay down to rest for just a moment, but I went to ____(sleep)____ .

MASTERY REQUIREMENT: 4 correct responses

Indicate mastery on the student response sheet with a check.

III. COMPREHENSION

    G.   Context Clues

© 1999 by The Center for Applied Research in Education, Inc.

Name _____

Date _____

Mastery _____

1. When you go out, please close the _____ quietly.

2. After we eat, we should always brush our

    _____ .

3. I am going to bake a big chocolate _____ for dessert.

4. The kitten climbed up to the top of the big pine

    _____ .

5. I lay down to rest for just a moment, but I went to

    _____ .

III.   COMPREHENSION   H.   Appropriate Title

OBJECTIVE: The student will select an appropriate title for a story.

SAY: Listen carefully as I read a story to you.

> One day our teacher told us all to bring a permission slip from home the next day saying that we could go on the bus to the wildlife museum in a near-by town. Our teacher asked the class if any of us had been there before. No one in the class had. The teacher thought we would really enjoy it, and that we would learn some interesting things, too.
>
> The next day we all got on the bus to go. When we got to the wildlife museum, many of us remembered that we had seen the building before; but we had never known what it was or what was in it.
>
> When we all were inside the front door in the waiting room, we were met by a woman who said that she was to be our guide. She said if we would stay together and listen to her she would explain the displays to us and then give us a chance to ask questions about what we saw. Many of us still didn't really know what we were going to see. As we started down the first hall, we saw that each wall was made out of glass. Behind the glass were many animals. Each animal was in a little place with grass, trees, stones, and water around it. We thought it was all real at first. Then our guide explained that these animals were all stuffed. She told us that people who stuff animals like that are called taxi-dermists. Those animals certainly did look alive, even if they were not. Many animals that live in our state were shown in the museum. The stones, grass, trees, and water were there to show the kind of place in which each animal lived.
>
> It took three hours to see all the animals that were on display in the museum, but it was so interesting none of us became tired.

SAY: Now look at your paper. Read these titles to yourself as I read them aloud. They all might be used as a title to the story you just heard. Some are good titles and some would not be very good. Mark an X in the blank by the two titles that you think are best.

_____   1.   Our Teacher

__x__   2.   An Interesting School Trip

_____   3.   Permission Slips

__x__   4.   A Morning at the Wildlife Museum

_____   5.   What Taxidermists Do

_____   6.   A Bus Ride

MASTERY REQUIREMENT: Two correct; no others marked.

Indicate mastery on the student response sheet with a check.

FIRST LEVEL

III. COMPREHENSION

H. Appropriate Title

Name _____

Date _____

Mastery _____

_____ 1. Our Teacher

_____ 2. An Interesting School Trip

_____ 3. Permission Slips

_____ 4. A Morning at the Wildlife Museum

_____ 5. What Taxidermists Do

_____ 6. A Bus Ride

III. COMPREHENSION   I. Relate Story Content to Own Experiences

OBJECTIVE: The student will relate the content of stories to his or her own experiences.

SAY: Read this story to yourself as I read it aloud.

> Debbie and Diane knew they were in trouble. They had not done it on purpose; it was an accident. But they had been careless. If they had been careful, it would not have happened. There was no way they could fix it so that no one would find out.
>
> They heard their parents coming in the door. Oh, they were going to be mad when they saw what had happened!

SAY: Now I want you to tell me a true story about something that has happened to you.

DIRECTIONS: Use student response sheet to record your assessment of the quality of the response given by the student.

MASTERY REQUIREMENT: Teacher judgment

Indicate mastery on the student response sheet with a check.

III. COMPREHENSION

    I. Relate Story Content
        to Own Experiences

Name _____

Date _____

Mastery _____

Debbie and Diane knew they were in trouble. They had not done it on purpose; it was an accident. But they had been careless. If they had been careful, it would not have happened. There was no way they could fix it so that no one would find out.

They heard their parents coming in the door. Oh, they were going to be mad when they saw what had happened!

Teacher assessment _____

_____

_____

IV. ORAL AND SILENT READING SKILLS   A. Oral Reading   1. Pronunciation

OBJECTIVE: The student will display adequate pronunciation skills in oral reading.

DIRECTIONS: Have the student read the sentences aloud. Mark your appraisal of punctuation correctness on the student response sheet.

SAY: Read these sentence aloud to me.

1. Terry is going to give me something.

2. Jackie batted four times in the game.

3. Isn't that a pretty Christmas tree?

4. Thank you for the surprise.

5. Which way do we walk to get to the apple tree?

MASTERY REQUIREMENT: A rating of "Fair" or better

Indicate mastery on the student response sheet with a check.

IV.   ORAL AND SILENT
       READING SKILLS

Name _____

     A.   Oral Reading

Date _____

          1.   Pronunciation

Mastery _____

1.   Terry is going to give me something.

2.   Jackie batted four times in the game.

3.   Isn't that a pretty Christmas tree?

4.   Thank you for the surprise.

5.   Which way do we walk to get to the apple tree?

Teacher assessment of pronunciation: _____ excellent

_____ good

_____ fair

_____ poor

Comment: _____

_____

IV. ORAL AND SILENT READING SKILLS   A.   Oral Reading   2.   Phrasing

OBJECTIVE: The student will use correct phrasing (not word-by-word) in oral reading.

DIRECTIONS: Have the student read the sentences aloud. Mark your appraisal on the student response sheet.

SAY: Read these sentences aloud to me.

1.   Tim wore a cowboy suit to the party.

2.   The elm tree in our back yard fell.

3.   James can work on the farm.

4.   I think that puppy belongs to Martha.

5.   The kitten jumped up on the table.

MASTERY REQUIREMENT: A rating of "Fair" or better

Indicate mastery on the student response sheet with a check.

IV. **ORAL AND SILENT READING SKILLS**

    A. **Oral Reading**

        2. **Phrasing**

Name _____

Date _____

Mastery _____

1. Tim wore a cowboy suit to the party.

2. The big elm tree in our back yard fell.

3. James can work on the farm.

4. I think that puppy belongs to Martha.

5. The kitten jumped up on the table.

Teacher assessment of phrasing: ____ excellent

                         ____ good

                         ____ fair

                         ____ poor

Comment: _____

IV.   ORAL AND SILENT READING SKILLS   A.   Oral Reading   3.   Voice intonation

OBJECTIVE: When reading orally, the student will use voice intonation to give meaning to material read.

DIRECTIONS: Have the student read the sentences aloud. Mark your appraisal of voice intonation on the student response sheet.

SAY: Read these sentences aloud to me.

1.   Mother asked why I was so late.

2.   Where is Tom?

3.   Linda, come here right now.

4.   Dad, please take us fishing this afternoon.

5.   Wait just a minute. I'm coming as fast as I can.

MASTERY REQUIREMENT: A rating of "Fair" or better

Indicate mastery on the student response sheet with a check.

FIRST LEVEL

IV. **ORAL AND SILENT**
   READING SKILLS

   A. **Oral Reading**

      3. **Voice intonation**

Name _____

Date _____

Mastery _____

1. Mother asked why I was so late.

2. Where is Tom?

3. Linda, come here right now.

4. Dad, please take us fishing this afternoon.

5. Wait just a minute. I'm coming as fast as I can.

Teacher assessment of voice intonation: _____ excellent

_____ good

_____ fair

_____ poor

Comment: _____

IV. ORAL AND SILENT READING SKILLS   A. Oral Reading   4. Posture and book handling

OBJECTIVE: The student will demonstrate good posture and book handling during oral reading.

DIRECTIONS: Use any daily activity when the student is reading from a book orally to judge this objective. Mark your appraisal on the student response sheet.

MASTERY REQUIREMENT: A rating of "Fair" or better

Indicate mastery on the student response sheet with a check.

IV. ORAL AND SILENT
     READING SKILLS

    A. Oral Reading

        4. Posture and book
            handling

Name _____

Date _____

Mastery _____

Teacher assessment of posture and book handling:

_____ excellent

_____ good

_____ fair

_____ poor

Comment: _____

_____

IV. ORAL AND SILENT READING SKILLS   A. Oral Reading   5. Punctuation

OBJECTIVE: In oral reading, the student will demonstrate understanding of the period, comma, question mark, and exclamation mark.

DIRECTIONS: Have the student read the sentences aloud. On the student response sheet mark your appraisal of the appropriateness with which the student "reads in" the various punctuation marks.

SAY: Read these sentences aloud to me.

1. Mary is going to the store. Are you going with her?

2. If we win today, we must play again Friday.

3. Stop it! That hurts!

4. Oh, no! Are Bob, Sue, and Peggy all sick?

5. Look at that light at the top of the hill, Don.

MASTERY REQUIREMENT: A rating of "Fair" or better on each item

Indicate mastery on the student response sheet with a check.

IV. ORAL AND SILENT
    READING SKILLS

Name _____

  A. Oral Reading

Date _____

    5. Punctuation

Mastery _____

1. Mary is going to the store. Are you going with her?

2. If we win today, we must play again Friday.

3. Stop it! That hurts!

4. Oh, no! Are Bob, Sue, and Peggy all sick?

5. Look at that light at the top of the hill, Don.

Teacher assessments:

(.) _____ excellent
    _____ good
    _____ fair
    _____ poor

(,) _____ excellent
    _____ good
    _____ fair
    _____ poor

(?) _____ excellent
    _____ good
    _____ fair
    _____ poor

(!) _____ excellent
    _____ good
    _____ fair
    _____ poor

Comment: _____

_____

IV. ORAL AND SILENT READING SKILLS   A. Oral Reading   5. Punctuation

a. period

OBJECTIVE: In oral reading, the student will demonstrate understanding of the period.

DIRECTIONS: Have student read the following aloud. On the student response sheet mark your appraisal of the appropriateness with which the student "reads in" the periods.

SAY: Read this aloud to me.

Jean is going to go to the zoo on Friday. Mother said I could go with her if I come right home after school. I will not stop on my way home that day. Going to the zoo is always fun. Maybe we can stay a long time.

MASTERY REQUIREMENT: A rating of "Fair" or better

Indicate mastery on the student response sheet with a check.

IV. ORAL AND SILENT
READING SKILLS

   A. Oral Reading

      5. Punctuation

         a. period

Name _____

Date _____

Mastery _____

Jean is going to go to the zoo on Friday. Mother said I could go with her if I come right home after school. I will not stop on my way home that day. Going to the zoo is always fun. Maybe we can stay a long time.

Teacher assessment: _____ excellent

                                _____ good

                                _____ fair

                                _____ poor

Comment: _____

_____

FIRST LEVEL

IV. ORAL AND SILENT READING SKILLS   A. Oral Reading   5. Punctuation

b. comma

OBJECTIVE: In oral reading, the student will demonstrate understanding of the comma.

DIRECTIONS: Have student read the following aloud. On the student response sheet mark your appraisal of the appropriateness with which the student "reads in" the commas.

SAY: Read this aloud to me.

Jerry, we must hurry or we will be late. If we are not there by two o'clock, we will miss the first of the movie. Tom, Joan, Eric, and Allison said they would wait for us at the corner. If we are late, they will go on without us.

MASTERY REQUIREMENT: A rating of "Fair" or better

Indicate mastery on the student response sheet with a check.

IV. ORAL AND SILENT
     READING SKILLS

    A. Oral Reading

        5. Punctuation

           b. comma

Name _____

Date _____

Mastery _____

Jerry, we must hurry or we will be late. If we are not there by two o'clock, we will miss the first of the movie. Tom, Joan, Eric, and Allison said they would wait for us at the corner. If we are late, they will go on without us.

Teacher assessment: _____ excellent

                                _____ good

                                _____ fair

                                _____ poor

Comment: _____

_____

IV. ORAL AND SILENT READING SKILLS   A. Oral Reading   5. Punctuation

                                                                      c. question
mark

OBJECTIVE: In oral reading, the student will demonstrate understanding of the question mark.

DIRECTIONS: Have student read the following aloud. On the student response sheet mark your appraisal of the appropriateness with which the student "reads in" the question marks.

SAY: Read this aloud to me.

      Ken, do you think your mother and father will let you spend the night with me? We will watch the football game on TV. Do you know who is playing? We can stay up late because it is Friday. On school nights, what time do you have to go to bed?

MASTERY REQUIREMENT: A rating of "Fair" or better

Indicate mastery on the student response sheet with a check.

IV. **ORAL AND SILENT READING SKILLS**

    A. **Oral Reading**

        5. **Punctuation**

            c. **question mark**

Name _____

Date _____

Mastery _____

Ken, do you think your mother and father will let you spend the night with me? We will watch the football game on TV. Do you know who is playing? We can stay up late because it is Friday. On school nights, what time do you have to go to bed?

Teacher assessment: _____ excellent

                              _____ good

                              _____ fair

                              _____ poor

Comment: _____

_____

IV. ORAL AND SILENT READING SKILLS   A. Oral Reading   5. Punctuation

                                                                              d. exclamation
                                                                                  mark

OBJECTIVE: In oral reading, the student will demonstrate understanding of the exclamation mark.

DIRECTIONS: Have student read the following aloud. On the student response sheet mark your appraisal of the appropriateness with which the student "reads in" the exclamation marks.

SAY: Read this aloud to me.

        Stop it! If you do that any more; you will tear the page out of the book. Oh, no! It is already torn. Quick! Hide it before Miss Ray comes back and sees it. Here she comes down the hall. Hurry, Jim! Hurry!

MASTERY REQUIREMENT: A rating of "Fair" or better

Indicate mastery on the student response sheet wit a check.

IV. **ORAL AND SILENT**
     READING SKILLS

    A. Oral Reading

       5. Punctuation

          d. exclamation mark

Name _____

Date _____

Mastery _____

Stop it! If you do that any more, you will tear the page out of the book. Oh no! It is already torn. Quick! Hide it before Miss Ray comes back and sees it. Here she comes down the hall. Hurry, Jim! Hurry!

Teacher assessment: _____ excellent

                            _____ good

                            _____ fair

                            _____ poor

Comment: _____

_____

IV. ORAL AND SILENT READING SKILLS   B. Silent Reading   1. Reads without vocalization

a. lip movements
b. whispering

OBJECTIVE: When engaged in silent reading, the student will read without lip movements or whispering.

DIRECTIONS: Use any daily opportunities to observe students for this objective. The appraisal should be made during a time the student is reading material in which all or nearly all of the words are familiar.

MASTERY REQUIREMENT: Demonstrated ability to read familiar material without vocalization in the form of lip movement or whispering

Indicate mastery on the student response sheet with a check.

IV. ORAL AND SILENT
    READING SKILLS

    B. Silent Reading

        1. Reads Without
           Vocalization

           a. lip movements
           b. whispering

Name _____

Date _____

Mastery _____

Comment: _____

_____

_____

IV. ORAL AND SILENT READING SKILLS   B.   Silent Reading   2.   Head
                                                                        movements

OBJECTIVE: When engaged in silent reading, the student will read without head move-
               ments.

DIRECTIONS: Use any daily activity to observe students on this objective. The appraisal
               should be made at a time when the student is unaware of being watched and
               should be made not only on book reading, but also on reading from the chalk-
               board.

MASTERY REQUIREMENT: Demonstrated ability to read without head movement from
                      books and from chalkboard

Indicate mastery on the student response sheet with a check.

FIRST LEVEL

IV. ORAL AND SILENT
    READING SKILLS

    B.   Silent Reading

        2.   Head movements

Name _____

Date _____

Mastery _____

Comment: _____

_____

_____

Name of Teacher: _____

GROUP SUMMARY PROFILE FIRST LEVEL

Student Names

	I. Vocabulary:	**A.** Word Recognition	1. Recognizes words with both upper and lower-case letters at beginning	2. Knows names of letters in sequence	3. Is able to identify in various settings words usually found in preprimers and primers	**II.** Word Analysis:	**A.** Sound-symbol Association	1. Associates consonant sounds	2. Names letters to represent consonant sounds	a. Initial position	b. Final position	c. Medial position	3. Discriminates between words	a. Initial letter cues	b. Final letter cues	4. Associates sounds to digraphs	5. Associates sounds to two letter blends	6. Knows that the letters a, e, i, o, u, and combinations of these can represent several different sounds	**B.** Structural Analysis	1. Knows endings	a. ed sound as "ed" in wanted	b. ed sound as "d" in moved	c. ed sound as "t" in liked	2. Recognizes compound words	3. Knows common word families	**C.** Word Form Clues	1. Recognizes upper and lower-case letters

School: _____ Year: _____

	2. Recognizes words of different length
	3. Recognizes words with double letters
	III. Comprehension
	A. Understands that printed symbols represent objects or actions
	B. Can follow printed directions
	C. Can draw conclusions from given facts
	D. Can recall from stories read aloud:
	1. Main idea
	2. Names of characters
	3. Important details
	4. Stated sequence
	E. Can recall after silent reading:
	1. Main idea
	2. Names of characters
	3. Important details
	4. Stated sequence
	F. Can distinguish between real and imaginary events
	G. Uses context clues in word attack
	H. Can suggest or select an appropriate title for a story
	I. Can relate story content to own experiences
	IV. Oral and Silent Reading Skills
	A. Oral Reading
	1. Uses correct pronunciation
	2. Uses correct phrasing (not word-by-word)
	3. Uses proper voice intonation to give meaning
	4. Has good posture and handles book appropriately
	5. Understands simple punctuation:
	a. Period
	b. Comma
	c. Question mark
	d. Exclamation mark
	B. Silent Reading
	1. Reads without vocalization
	2. Reads without head movements

Name of Teacher: _____

GROUP
SUMMARY
PROFILE
FIRST LEVEL

Student Names

	I. Vocabulary:	A. Word Recognition	1. Recognizes words with both upper and lower-case letters at beginning	2. Knows names of letters in sequence	3. Is able to identify in various settings words usually found in preprimers and primers	II. Word Analysis:	A. Sound-symbol Association	1. Associates consonant sounds	2. Names letters to represent consonant sounds	a. Initial position	b. Final position	c. Medial position	3. Discriminates between words	a. Initial letter cues	b. Final letter cues	4. Associates sounds to digraphs	5. Associates sounds to two letter blends	6. Knows that the letters a, e, i, o, u, and combinations of these can represent several different sounds	B. Structural Analysis	1. Knows endings	a. ed sound as "ed" in wanted	b. ed sound as "d" in moved	c. ed sound as "t" in liked	2. Recognizes compound words	3. Knows common word families	C. Word Form Clues	1. Recognizes upper and lower-case letters

School: _____ Year: _____

2. Recognizes words of different length
3. Recognizes words with double letters
III. **Comprehension**
A. **Understands that printed symbols represent objects or actions**
B. **Can follow printed directions**
C. **Can draw conclusions from given facts**
D. **Can recall from stories read aloud:**
1. Main idea
2. Names of characters
3. Important details
4. Stated sequence
E. **Can recall after silent reading:**
1. Main idea
2. Names of characters
3. Important details
4. Stated sequence
F. **Can distinguish between real and imaginary events**
G. **Uses context clues in word attack**
H. **Can suggest or select an appropriate title for a story**
I. **Can relate story content to own experiences**
IV. **Oral and Silent Reading Skills**
A. **Oral Reading**
1. Uses correct pronunciation
2. Uses correct phrasing (not word-by-word)
3. Uses proper voice intonation to give meaning
4. Has good posture and handles book appropriately
5. Understands simple punctuation:
  a. Period
  b. Comma
  c. Question mark
  d. Exclamation mark
B. **Silent Reading**
1. Reads without vocalization
2. Reads without head movements

Name of Teacher: _____

GROUP
SUMMARY
PROFILE
FIRST LEVEL

Student Names

I. **Vocabulary:**

A. **Word Recognition**
1. Recognizes words with both upper and lower-case letters at beginning
2. Knows names of letters in sequence
3. Is able to identify in various settings words usually found in preprimers and primers

II. **Word Analysis:**

A. **Sound-symbol Association**
1. Associates consonant sounds
2. Names letters to represent consonant sounds
   a. Initial position
   b. Final position
   c. Medial position
3. Discriminates between words
   a. Initial letter cues
   b. Final letter cues
4. Associates sounds to digraphs
5. Associates sounds to two letter blends
6. Knows that the letters a, e, i, o, u, and combinations of these can represent several different sounds

B. **Structural Analysis**
1. Knows endings
   a. ed sound as "ed" in wanted
   b. ed sound as "d" in moved
   c. ed sound as "t" in liked
2. Recognizes compound words
3. Knows common word families

C. **Word Form Clues**
1. Recognizes upper and lower-case letters

2. Recognizes words of different length

3. Recognizes words with double letters

III. Comprehension

A. Understands that printed symbols represent objects or actions

B. Can follow printed directions

C. Can draw conclusions from given facts

D. Can recall from stories read aloud:

1. Main idea

2. Names of characters

3. Important details

4. Stated sequence

E. Can recall after silent reading:

1. Main idea

2. Names of characters

3. Important details

4. Stated sequence

F. Can distinguish between real and imaginary events

G. Uses context clues in word attack

H. Can suggest or select an appropriate title for a story

I. Can relate story content to own experiences

IV. Oral and Silent Reading Skills

A. Oral Reading

1. Uses correct pronunciation

2. Uses correct phrasing (not word-by-word)

3. Uses proper voice intonation to give meaning

4. Has good posture and handles book appropriately

5. Understands simple punctuation:

a. Period

b. Comma

c. Question mark

d. Exclamation mark

B. Silent Reading

1. Reads without vocalization

2. Reads without head movements